Pope Francis

Religious Leader

by Grace Hansen

ABDO
HISTORY MAKER
BIOGRAPHIES
Kids

abdopublishing.com

Published by Abdo Kids, a division of ABDO, PO Box 398166, Minneapolis, Minnesota 55439.

Copyright © 2015 by Abdo Consulting Group, Inc. International copyrights reserved in all countries. No part of this book may be reproduced in any form without written permission from the publisher.

Printed in the United States of America, North Mankato, Minnesota.

102014

012015

THIS BOOK CONTAINS RECYCLED MATERIALS

Photo Credits: AP Images, Corbis, iStock, Shutterstock

Production Contributors: Teddy Borth, Jennie Forsberg, Grace Hansen

Design Contributors: Laura Rask, Dorothy Toth

Library of Congress Control Number: 2014943710

Cataloging-in-Publication Data

Hansen, Grace.

 Pope Francis: religious leader / Grace Hansen.

   p. cm. -- (History maker biographies)

Includes index.

ISBN 978-1-62970-705-1

1. Francis, Pope, 1936- --Juvenile literature. 2. Popes --Argentina--Biography--Juvenile literature.

1. Title.

282/.092--dc23

[B]

2014943710

Table of Contents

Jorge Bergoglio

Jorge Bergoglio was born on December 17, 1936. He was born in Buenos Aires, Argentina. He would one day be Pope Francis.

North America

South America

Argentina

Buenos Aires

Jorge was very smart.

He did well in science.

He played soccer for fun.

He also liked to dance.

Becoming a Priest

At age 17, Jorge went to church.

He got a message from God.

It was to become a priest.

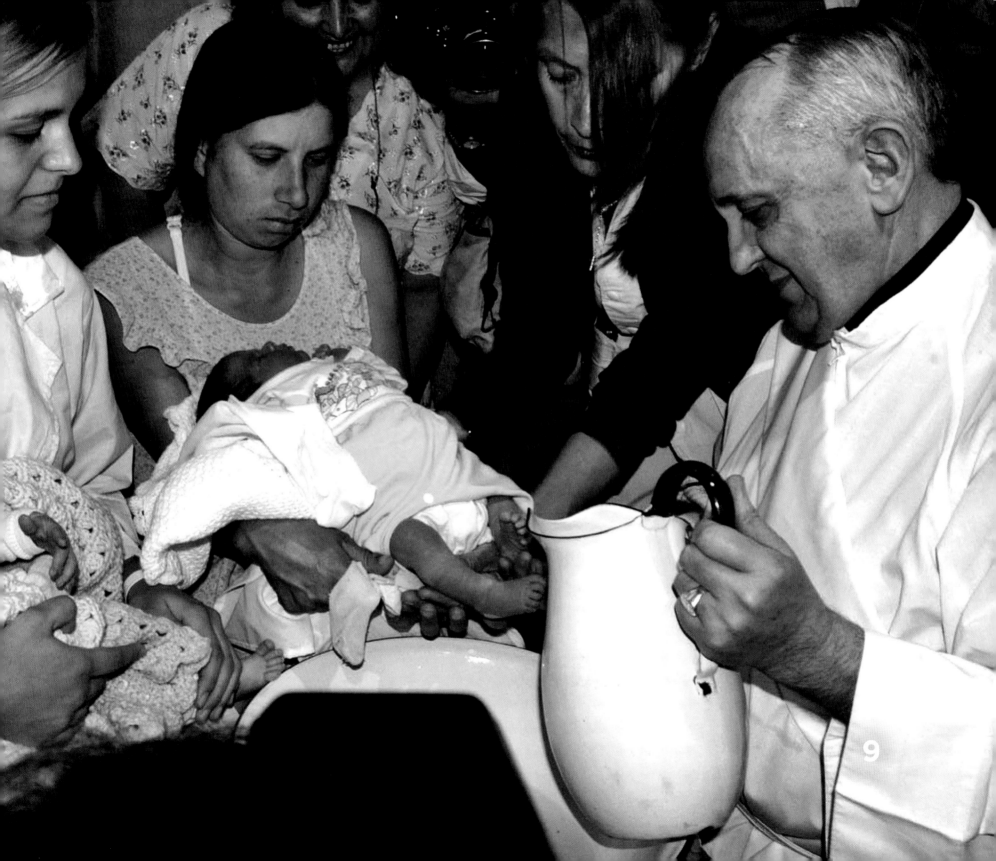

In 1960, Jorge took his **Jesuit** vows. He was just 24 years old. He studied a lot. Jesuits care very much about education.

11

Teaching

Jorge hoped to travel. He wanted to help the poor. Instead, he was asked to teach. He taught for 3 years. In 1969, he became a **Jesuit** priest.

13

Becoming Pope Francis

In 1992, Jorge was made auxiliary bishop. He helped the **archbishop** of Buenos Aires. Pope John Paul II gave him this title.

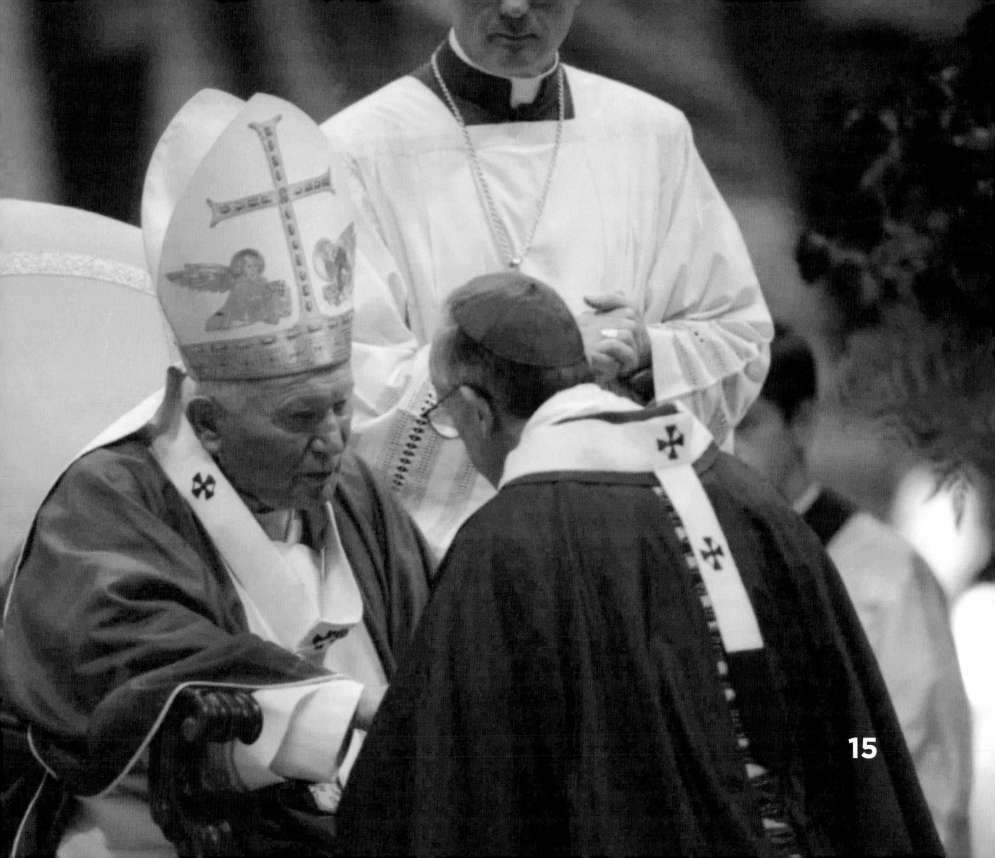

In 1998, the **archbishop** of Buenos Aires died. Jorge took his place. In 2001, he became a **cardinal**, too.

16

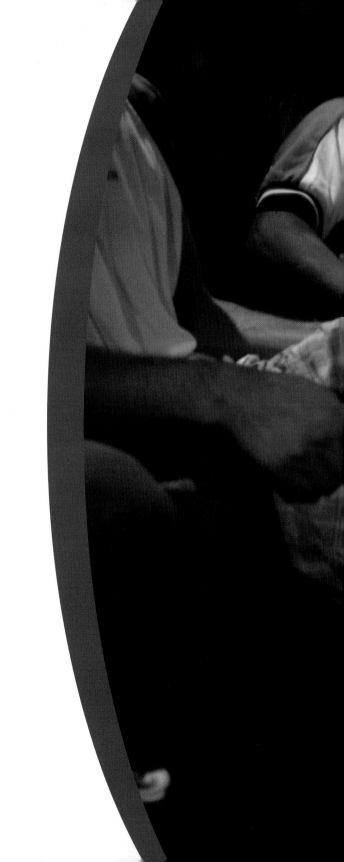

Jorge could have lived in a nice home. He could have had nice things. But he still chose a life of **poverty**. He cared more about helping the poor and sick.

18

19

On March 13, 2013, Jorge was elected pope. Jorge took the name Francis. This is after St. Francis of Assisi. Pope Francis is loved by many.

21

Timeline

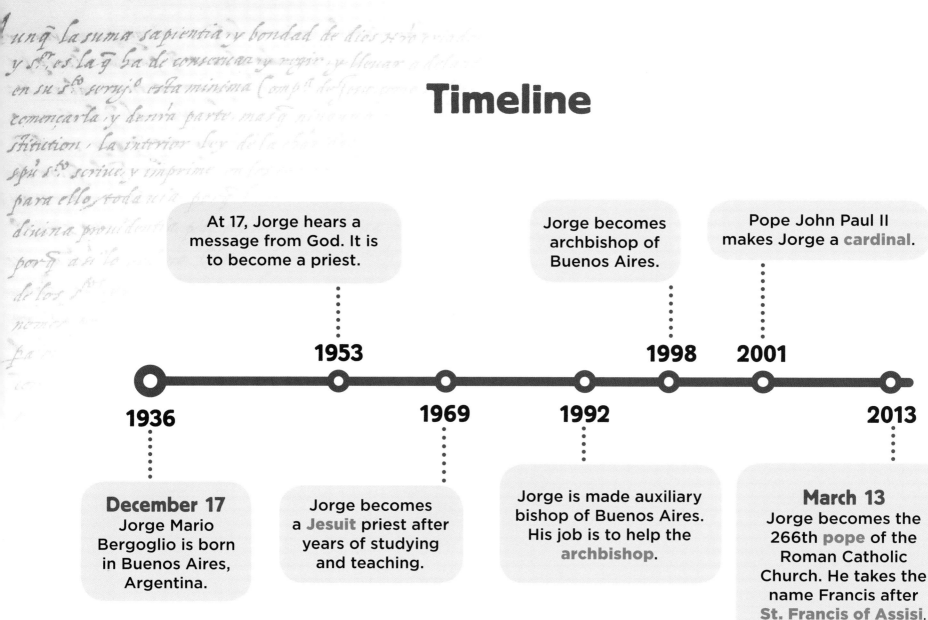

At 17, Jorge hears a message from God. It is to become a priest.

Jorge becomes archbishop of Buenos Aires.

Pope John Paul II makes Jorge a **cardinal**.

1953

1998 **2001**

1936

1969 **1992** **2013**

December 17
Jorge Mario Bergoglio is born in Buenos Aires, Argentina.

Jorge becomes a **Jesuit** priest after years of studying and teaching.

Jorge is made auxiliary bishop of Buenos Aires. His job is to help the **archbishop**.

March 13
Jorge becomes the 266th **pope** of the Roman Catholic Church. He takes the name Francis after **St. Francis of Assisi**.

Glossary

archbishop – someone who is in charge of church matters in a large geological area. An auxiliary bishop helps the archbishop.

cardinal – someone who is nominated by the pope and helps decide who becomes the next pope. All cardinals are also bishops or archbishops.

Jesuit – a member of the Society of Jesus who is devoted to missionary and educational work.

pope – the bishop of Rome and the head of the Roman Catholic Church.

poverty – the state of lacking money and material possessions.

St. Francis of Assisi – a saint who lived in the 1100s. He gave away all of his money and belongings, and devoted himself to the poor. He believed in living a simple and peaceful life.

Index

abdokids.com

Use this code to log on to abdokids.com and access crafts, games, videos, and more!

Abdo Kids Code:
HPK7051